HANDCART TO H*   N

1st Edition

Published in 2013 by
Woodfield Publishing Ltd
Bognor Regis PO21 5EL England
www.woodfieldpublishing.co.uk

Copyright © 2013 Brian Janman

All rights reserved

This publication is protected by international law. No part of its contents may be copied, reproduced or transmitted in any form or by any means, electronic or mechanical, or be stored in any information storage & retrieval system, without prior permission in writing from Woodfield Publishing Ltd

The right of Brian Janman to be identified as author of this work has been asserted in accordance with the Copyright, Designs and Patents Act 1988

ISBN 1-84683-158-X

Printed and bound in England

Handcart to Hanlon

West Sussex Ambulance Services 1885-1995

WEST SUSSEX LIBRARY SERVICE	
20	226668
For	2/14
362.188	

Woodfield

Woodfield Publishing Ltd
Bognor Regis ~ West Sussex ~ England ~ PO21 5EL
tel 01243 821234 ~ **e/m** info@woodfieldpublishing.co.uk

Interesting and informative books on a variety of subjects

For full details of all our published titles, visit our website at
www.woodfieldpublishing.co.uk

This book is dedicated to all the ambulance men and women who have served the people of West Sussex

Acknowledgements

The author is indebted to all those who so generously loaned or donated the photographs and provided the information used in compiling this history. Without them it would have been impossible to produce. They include:

West Sussex Ambulance Service, West Sussex Ambulance Service Archives, West Sussex Ambulance Service Retirement Association, Sussex Ambulance Service NHS Trust, The St John Ambulance Divisions and British Red Cross Society Centres of West Sussex, West Sussex Record Office, West Sussex County Library Service, East Sussex Record Office, The British Red Cross Museum & Archives, The Museum of the Order of St John, The National Motor Museum, East Grinstead Museum, Henfield Museum, Worthing Museum, Littlehampton Museum, Steyning Museum , Bognor Post, West Sussex County Times, Observer Newspaper Group, Worthing Gazette, Worthing Herald, Sussex Newspapers, Promoter Newspaper, Wadham Stringer Ltd, Caffyns Garage.

along with:

Pat Weeks, Sid Lacey, Doreen Sampson, Brian Knight, Stan Linstead , Allan Ware, Ken Smith, Dennis Highfield, Roger Farley, Peter Wells, Tim Murgatroyd, Gordon Lenthall, Mr. H.K.Moody, John Layhe, Wally Field, Frank Holmes, Andy Brian, Jack Thompson, Bert Selsby, Goff Tame, Eric Huntingdon, Jim Parker, Vince Glover, Nigel Smith, Vince Shaw, Gordon Clare, Mrs Smith, Margaret Terry, Mrs. Moles, Mrs Janet Greener, Mrs J Skaptason, Bob Reid, Jim Vincent, Mrs Parker, Collin Keywood, Brian Jones, Stan & Sandra Skinner, Richard Southgate, Ron Iden, Wilf Virgo, Roger Saych, Ron Parsons, Floss Mitchell, Peter Williams.

Every effort has been made to ensure the accuracy of the contents of his book and credit the copyholders of the photographs included. In addition to the acknowledgements above, a large proportion of the photographs have come from the authors own collection.

My special thanks go to members of the Ambulance Heritage Society for helping me with identifying the make and model of many of the earlier ambulances illustrated.

Foreword

With the demise of many county ambulance services across the country through amalgamation, the history of most services have and are being lost forever. By compiling the history and development of the Ambulances Services of West Sussex, Brian has managed to capture the essence of those services and the people who served in them.

The evolution of the ambulance service from the late 1800s to the Paramedic service of today only came about through the dedication of the men and women who have provided the care and commitment to the community of West Sussex across the years.

The advances in medical knowledge and equipment over time have had a dramatic effect on ambulance staffs ability to treat sick and injured patients. The days when all the equipment carried on ambulances was a few triangular bandages, some wooden splints and of course a bedpan, have long gone.

One only has to look at the advances in resuscitation to see just how much things have changed. From Eve's Rocking method to the Silvester method where we pressed on the patient's lower back in an attempt to expel air and ventilate the lungs, and then with the Holger Nielsen method we tried pressing down on the chest with the patient's arms and then raising them to try to expand the chest cavity. Finally along came Mouth to Mouth and we were given a Brook Airway (a one way blow-pipe!) By 1995 we had established the first paramedic training in the county and we were routinely intubating patients and also infusing those who had suffered blood loss. A far cry from the early days.

What has not changed over all these years was the camaraderie which existed between the staff. I have served in several ambulance services during my career, but in West Sussex the friendliness of the staff and the feeling of being in one family was palpable.

Our gratitude goes to Brain for compiling the history of the West Sussex Ambulance Services for future generations.

Ken Smith. O.OSt
Chief Ambulance Officer, West Sussex Ambulance Service 1989-1995

References

Ambulances.	Chris Batten, 1996
Ambulance Handbook 6th edition.	George Thomas Beaton, 1898
First Aid to the Sick & Injured 17th Edition	Warwick & Tunstall, 1939
NHS Ambulances, The First 25 years.	Chris Batten, 1998
Now Another Pharaoh.	P.R. Thatcher, 1988
St.John Ambulance Crawley Division 1928-52, A Short History.	Simon Redhead
St.John Ambulance Horsham Division 1906 - 1926 - 1976, A History	Frank Holmes
St.John Ambulance Littlehampton, A Short History.	W.R. Kemp
St.John in Focus.	Museum of the Order of St.John of Jerusalem, London, 1987
The Ambulance.	Katherine Traver Barrkley, 1990
The Red Cross Then and Now.	Richard Cavendish, 1984
The Health of the County annual reports.	WSCC, 1961-1972

Introduction

I joined the Ambulance Service in 1975 by the simple expedient of walking into the ambulance station in Bognor Regis one day and asking if there were any jobs going. By chance there were, and after an interview I found myself starting a new job just a few weeks later - they were fussy in those days you know! Just why I applied remains a mystery to me to this day, as I had never had the slightest inclination towards this type of work before, but it turned out to be one of the best decisions I ever made

1. The author, 1976.

It was in the mid eighties that I began to take a serious interest in the history of the ambulance service in West Sussex, most likely as a result of the Sunday morning chat sessions round the crew room table, being told tales of daring do by the stations old timers. Before long I had started to collect a few old photographs and other odds and sods, and before I knew it I had the beginnings of an archive. This grew and grew as I went round the counties libraries, record offices and newspaper archives digging out more and more information, and as word of my strange endeavours spread, people began to send me old photos, even from as far away as Yorkshire. After a few years of this I thought that I had enough material to contemplate putting it all together in book form, but fate took a hand and I had to put the project aside for a few years.

The impetus to get the project going again came after I had to retire from my career as a Paramedic in 2009. I joined the West Sussex Ambulance Service Retirement Association and found myself sitting round a table again, albeit this time a pub one, chewing over the old days with some of my ex colleagues. The age of computers having well and truly arrived some 10 years earlier, along with the advent of the internet, made researching a very different game from the first time round, but it also meant having to spend a lot of time transferring photographs and paper data onto my computer. This did at least make the final compilation of the book a great deal easier; isn't technology a wonderful thing!

Needless to say I could not have put this volume together without the generosity shown by many people, especially those in the ambulance service or retired from it, who either gave me or lent me the vast majority of the photographs contained in it. Their work over the years treating and transporting the sick and injured of this county generally goes without remark - unless it is the much heard classic "What took you so long to get here?" - so hopefully this volume will go some way to redressing that situation. Many, many people, male and female, paid or volunteer, have donned the mantle of care and overcome rain, sleet, snow and managerial pressures to go to the aid of those in need, and its not until you need them that you realise just what a magnificent job they do.

B Janman

Before The NHS

To find the beginnings of the organised, uniformed civilian first aid and ambulance services as we know them today we need to go back to the later half of the 19th century and the emergence of such organisations as the International Red Cross Society and the St.John Ambulance Association.

The British Red Cross Society

As a result of his experiences during the Franco-Prussian War Henri Durant, a citizen of Geneve, wrote a book, Un Souvenir de Solferino, published in 1862, in which he put forward the idea of raising organised 'relief societies' in countries all across Europe. These societies were to train and equip volunteers to support the military medical services in time of war.

In 1863 a group of businessmen joined Durant to form the International Committee on Aid to the Wounded, which in 1875, became the International Committee of the Red Cross. The British Red Cross Society was founded in 1870, soon after the outbreak of the Franco-Prussian War. Initially known as the National Society for Aid to the Sick and Wounded in War, and adopting the now famous red cross on a white background as its badge, the movement spread quickly across the country, and was renamed as the British Red Cross Society in 1905, the Sussex Branch being formed the same year.

The society sent surgeons, nurses and medical supplies abroad to various wars, setting up field hospitals and assisting with the repatriation and rehabilitation of the wounded. During the First World War it worked in conjunction with the Order of St.John, recruiting and training the Voluntary Aid Detachments used to reinforce the army's own medical services.

As well as helping to staff hospitals and clinics some Sussex branches of the society, including Midhurst, East Grinstead, Haywards Heath, Petworth, Uckfield, Arundel, Bognor and Aldingbourne, either operated their own ambulances or provided the volunteers to crew vehicles operated by other organisations. In 1934 for example a report states that ambulances operated or manned by the Society covered a total of 26,022 miles and conveyed 1,431 patients. Some detachments, for example Midhurst, continued to provide ambulance cover under an agency agreement right up to 1963, when the County Council took over the direct provision of an ambulance service throughout the entire county.

The St. John Ambulance Association

The British Order of St.John founded the St.John Ambulance Association on July 1st 1877 with the aim of instructing people in first aid to the Injured and the distribution of ambulance equipment, and within a short period of time centres had been established across the country, including some in factories, collieries and railway companies.

Funds to support the work were raised by public donations and annual subscriptions. 'Corps' of volunteers who had been taught first aid by the Association were formed, the first in London, and on St. John's Day in 1887 the St.John Ambulance Brigade was instituted as 'a voluntary civilian organisation for rendering assistance in cases of accident or sudden illness in civilian emergencies', and became the uniformed branch of the Order as we know it today. Sir John Furley, who devised the ubiquitous Furley Stretcher, became the Brigade's first Director.

The Bognor Centre of the St.John Ambulance Association was established in 1885 and in the same year opened a subscription list to obtain the money to purchase an 'ambulance van'. The centres annual report of 1897 states "that one had now been purchased, along with one horse to pull it, and that it will be housed by the Bognor Urban District Council"

Extract from the 1895 Annual Report of the Bognor Centre of the St.John Ambulance Association.

'In submitting the yearly statement the committee beg to say that they would be very glad to receive more contributions to the centre. As the lectures are now arranged under the County Council regulations, entailing very little expense to the candidates, it will be necessary to have a list of subscribers and donors to be able to send to the Headquarters of the Association the yearly tribute they expect from every centre, according to it's ability.

A good class was held at Yapton last November, all those who presented themselves for examination passing it most satisfactorily. The examiner, Dr C Smith (of Brighton) expressed himself very pleased with the way the class had been tutored, it was a great credit to the lecturer, Dr A B Collins (of Yapton), who had taken a great deal of trouble to make the members efficient.

A woman's 'First Aid' class was held in February, also one for men under the same lecturer and the whole of the former passed, only one of the men's class failing to satisfy the examiner, who was very pleased with the way both classes had been instructed. We are in hope of having more classes in the spring'.

As was normally the case in those days, people had to pay for their health care if they had the means to do so, and transport by ambulance was no exception. A report from Bognor in 1898 quotes some of these charges:

"The ambulance van is available for the transport of sick persons to and from the villages around Bognor within a radius of five miles at a rate of 2/- per mile (minimum charge 5/-, within the Urban Council District 5/- and to Chichester Infirmary 10/6."

The report goes on to say that in 'parish' cases the patient may be moved free of charge, and that the van can be used for infectious cases, but only if the patient pays for it to be disinfected afterwards!

Other areas, Henfield was one of them, formed ambulance clubs, and your annual subscription entitled you to transport to hospital at no extra charge.

An early First Aid Certificate awarded to Albert Taylor by the Bognor Regis Centre of the St.John Ambulance Association in April 1894. It bears the signatures of the Right Reverend Bishop Tuffnell (President), Mr A Whitehouse Strickland (Hon Secretary), Dr A B Collins (Surgeon Instructor) and Dr W F Simpson (Examiner).

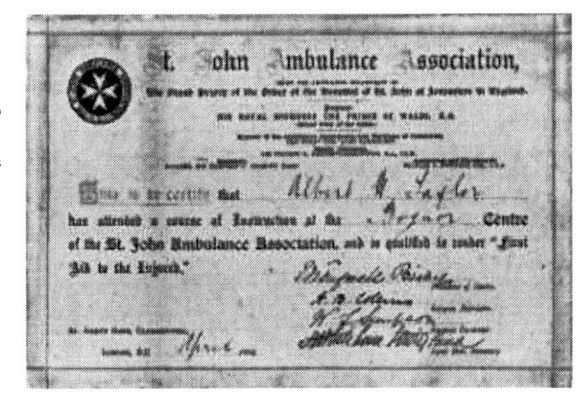

The Chichester St.John Division was first formed in about 1895 with its first headquarters in Crane Street, moving to rooms above the Buttermarket some when between 1900 and 1904. At first they had a wheeled stretcher and a bicycle ambulance. Almost the entire Men's Division joined the Army Medical Corps in the early months of The Great War; marching off to the railway station in full St.John uniform. Those who remained assisted the army in moving casualties from the railway station to the war hospital at Graylingwell.

2. Men of the Chichester St.John Ambulance Division formed up in the station yard at Chichester railway station before boarding the train to take them off to war.

The Chichester Division lay almost dormant after the war, those members still active assisting the Police who operated the city's ambulance at that time. The Division was revived in 1931 by Police Superintendent Brett and Dr Langhorne, initially holding its meetings at the Lancastrian School.

3. Chichester St.John Ambulance Brigade members loading a casualty into an ambulance outside Chichester railway station sometime during the Great War. An ambulance train had just brought wounded men from hospital ships to be taken to the local war hospitals, including Graylingwell. Note the canvas stretchers fitted to the side walls of the ambulance and the rolled up cover above the rear door.

The Littlehampton St.John Ambulance Division was formed at a meeting in the towns Auction Mart on Thursday July 29th 1897, and became fully incorporated into the Brigade in 1907. It purchased an Ashford Litter in 1911 at a cost of £16. During the First World War the Division made up a large part of the local VAD Detachment, and operated a Bean motor ambulance, fitted with solid tyres, on its behalf. The Division purchased its first motor ambulance, a Ford, in 1919 and by 1935 were operating a blue liveried Austin.

The Crawley Division was formed in 1928 by members of a Crawley and Three Bridges based Southern Railway first aid team, with help and encouragement from Dr Mathews (who became their first Divisional Surgeon) and Divisional Superintendent Jennings from the Horsham Division. Until the late 1940's the Division covered the horse racing meetings at Gatwick on what is now the site of the airport. One ambulance with crew and two other personnel were required for the duty, for which the charge was £2/10/0. They also manned roadside 'first aid boxes' at weekends.

The Southwick St.John Division was formed by 16 people during a meeting at Hove railway station in 1929, and by 1930 its members were manning the Shoreham Police Ambulance. The Division went through a series of name changes in its early years; at one time it was the Southwick, Shoreham and Portslade Division, before finally reverting to its original title of Southwick in 1946. The first ambulance the Division owned was an Arrol-Johnson, obtained from the Bexhill Division in 1942.

4. A First World War period Renault ambulance in Worthing.

The Horsham St.John Ambulance Association, formed in 1906 by six railway workers, initially held its classes in a platelayers hut in the marshalling yard in Horsham but was later given permission to use a waiting room at the station. There was no organised ambulance service; the only transport available was a wheeled litter which was borrowed from the local volunteer fire brigade. The West Sussex County Times reported on a public meeting held at Horsham Town Hall on June 26th 1926 when it was agreed to form a division of the St.John Ambulance Brigade in the town, and at the next meeting, held on July 6th, 30 qualified first aiders gave their names. In 1938 the Division was holding its meetings in the Town Hall and the ambulance was then kept in Jackson's Garage in Springfield Road. There was no accommodation for the duty crew, who waited for calls either by the garage telephone or on the corner of the Bishopric. The Division was able to build its own headquarters building in 1938.

The Home Ambulance Service

The British Red Cross and the Order of St.John formed the Joint War Committee early in the 1914-18 War to provide help to the armed services medical units. In 1919 they appointed a Home Service Ambulance Committee to set up a scheme to help the sick and injured in the UK. They arranged for serviceable ambulances to be returned from the battlefront and had them reconditioned in the Red Cross's own workshops. The Committee planned for County Directors to administer the scheme in their areas on a trial basis, but it soon became clear that a permanent service was needed, and ambulance stations were set up across the nation, equipped with these reconditioned vehicles, and crewed by trained volunteers. What became known as the Home Ambulance Service became this country's first nationwide ambulance service.

The ambulances were originally painted black and usually, but not always, carried both Red Cross and St.John wording, often written either side of a red cross on a white circle. The ambulances were often marked with the name of the town in which they were based. The service continued to operate throughout the Second World War, and In some areas into the early years of the Nation Health Service.

5. The wording on the side of this ambulance, a Model T Ford, photographed at around about the end of the Great War, says Littlehampton District Motor Ambulance. The vehicle carries both Red Cross and St.John logos, and is probably part of The Home Ambulance Service fleet.

Moody's Ambulance Service

Moody's Ambulance Service was started in the 1920's by Mr H.G Moody, the owner of a garage at the foot of Church Hill, Pulborough.

When an AA patrolman was knocked down on the nearby road junction by a steam lorry that had run down the hill out of control it took more than an hour for an ambulance reach him from Midhurst.

This incident prompted Mr Moony to learn first aid, taking lessons from a signalman at Pulborough railway station who was a member of the railways St.John Ambulance Division. He acquired a 38hp Daimler ambulance (left) and later went on to co-found the Pulborough Division of the St.John Ambulance Brigade.

6. Moody's Ambulance, Pulborough in the 1920's.

7. Mr Moody standing in front of his garage premises in the 1920's with one of his ambulances parked under the signboard.
Note the cans of petrol stacked up in the left foreground.

Police Ambulances

8. The St.John and Red Cross were not the only organisations to provide civilian ambulances. Police forces in Horsham, Shoreham and Worthing had their own, and several council health boards maintained separate 'fever ambulances' as well as ones for accident cases. The Horsham Police Ambulance pictured above c1926, and known as the 'Yellow Peril' (primarily because it was painted yellow but also because it was used to carry fever cases) was the town's first motor ambulance, and was kept at the Ford Works in Worthing Road. It was presented to the town by Mrs M Laughton JP at a ceremony in The Carfax on Saturday 18th September 1926, and accepted on behalf of the town by the Chief Constable, Mr A Williams.

The St.John Ambulance men are, from L/R, Reg Charman, Ben Street and Frank Fiest. The ambulance is a Morris Commercial.

FIRST AID

A new class for the instruction of First aid will start next week in connection with the Police, with vacancies for about six civilians.
Those wishing to join should communicate with Police-constable Abbott at the police Station.

Worthing Gazette 22nd October 1928

9. Presented to the Police by Mr H Aaron of Angmering-on-Sea, Worthing Police Ambulance No1, a Morris Commercial, pictured opposite the Police Station in Union Road in 1928, was driven by Police Officers and manned by St.John Ambulance Brigade volunteers.

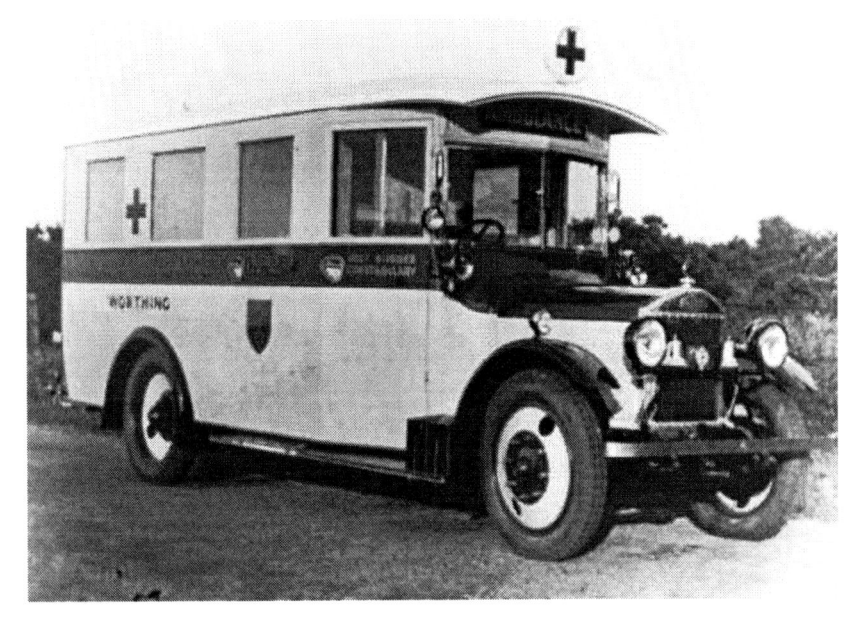

10. Worthing Police Ambulance No2, was based on a Dennis 30cwt chassis with bodywork by Caffyns of Horsham. Introduced in 1929, it was the second ambulance to be operated by the Worthing Police Ambulance Committee and was paid for by public subscription.

The Aeroplane Crash

11. Held in the grounds of the Bognor Regis War Memorial Hospital, this mock up of an aeroplane crash was staged on May 6th 1931 in the presence of Colonel Barry, a War Office Inspecting Officer, during the towns Red Cross Voluntary Aid Detachment's (Sussex 88) annual inspection.

12. Dedication ceremony for the Chichester St. John Ambulance Division's first motor ambulance, an Austin, in 1931.

13. Two Commer ambulances belonging to the Worthing St. John Ambulance Division outside their garages in the railway station yard, Southcoate Road. 1n 1933, when this picture was taken, the Division had 4 Officers, 4 Sergeants and Corporals and 37 Privates. The Division moved to 'Candia' in Farncombe Road in 1946.

PO 7268 was presented to the SJAB by the towns Mayor, Mr T.B. Hawkins in April 1933. BBP 24 had a body taken from a Napier ambulance purchased from the St. John Ambulance Brigade in Guildford, and rebuilt onto a new Commer chassis by Worthing SJAB members and nicknamed 'The Napier'.

14. Littlehampton St John Ambulance Brigade members manning a seafront First Aid Hut in the early 1930's.

15. Horsham St. John Ambulance Division's Lomas bodied 27hp Willy's Knight ambulance, purchased for £350 in 1929, in the yard at Jackson's Garage in Springfield Road in 1934. This was the first motor ambulance the division owned. Prior to this brigade members manned an ambulance operated by the town's police force (the 'Yellow Peril', page 8) The ambulanceman on the left is Frank Holmes.

16. Midhurst's first motor ambulance, a Morris, was converted from a car given to the town's Red Cross Detachment in 1932. The Officer in this 1935 photograph is probably Mr Melhuish, who ran the service until 1956, after which Cocking publican Vic Charman took over the day to day running of the ambulance, which was kept in a garage in Grange Road.

12

17. The Aldingbourne (Sussex 63) British Red Cross Detachment's Morris ambulance, registration number HW 3588, on the forecourt of what was then the Aldingbourne Village School in 1935. Mr Hoad, a signalman on the Southern Railway, was the unit's commanding officer. The ambulance was kept in the old Silver Queen bus garage in Fontwell Avenue, and the unit held it's meetings in the Labour In Vain Public House at the top end of Westgate Street.

18. The Pulborough and District Ambulance Service's ambulance based on a Bullnose Morris chassis, circa 1936.

19. The second Petworth Police Ambulance, a Ford Model A, reg no PO 7621, photographed in August 1935 outside Castles Garage in Park Road.

It was purchased by public subscription in July 1933 and replaced an earlier vehicle that transferred from Worthing in the late 1920's.

20. The Brighton, Hove and Worthing Airport Authority's ambulance at Shoreham Airfield c1935.

21. Members of the Bognor Red Cross Men's Detachment (Sussex 47) on a training exercise in October 1935.

14

In 1908 a suggestion was put forward to Henfield Parish Council by Captain Baxter, a keen first-aider, that they should obtain a wheeled stretcher for use in the village. A concert was held to raise the necessary funds and in 1909 a 'one man ambulance' was purchased at a cost of £16/7 /3. It was kept in the local fire station in the High Street and used by the Fire Brigade and others. It was last used in 1932 to take a lady who had collapsed in Station Road back to her house in West End Lane. The stretcher survives to this day and is kept in Henfield Museum.

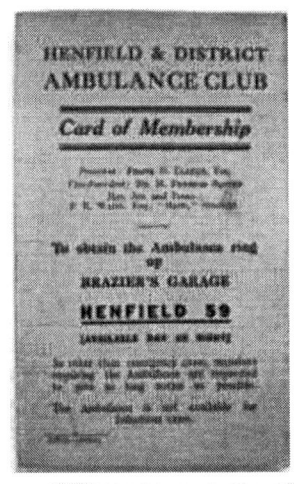

The Henfield and District Ambulance Club, was formed by Mr R B Rann and others in February 1934.
For an annual subscription of 1/6d the club provided a round-the-clock service, and by the end of its first year the club had 699 members.

22. St.John ambulance man John Brazier and his sister with the Henfield & District Ambulance Club's first motor ambulance on Henfield Common in 1935. It had been converted locally from a saloon car, which probably explains the highly unusual side door loading arrangements. It served the town until 1944 when it too was replaced with a second hand Austin ambulance.

23. Members of the Bognor Red Cross Detachment (Sussex 47) at the Jubilee Day Celebrations on the Hawthorn Road Recreation Ground, May 6th 1935. They took part in a joint demonstration with the towns Fire Brigade.

24. Bognor Urban District Council's Austin ambulance in the snow outside the Royal West Sussex Hospital in Chichester, January 1936.

25. Inset, the interior of the vehicles rear saloon.

26. Chichester St.John Ambulance Division members with two of their ambulances. On the left is an Austin Big 6 while the right hand vehicle is a Rolls Royce, donated to the Division by Dr Waring of Westgate.

27. Completed in 1938, Horsham St.John Division's new headquarters in Park Street was officially opened by Her Grace the Duchess of Norfolk in July 1939.

28. Crawley's St.John Ambulance Brigade was presented with its first ambulance, a Bedford, on May 21st 1933. It was a gift from Captain Wickham Noakes from Ifield, and was dedicated in front of a large crowd at the recreation ground on Three Bridges Road by Reverend Baynes. By 1937 this ambulance had done over 27,000 miles, had carried 763 patients and was in need of replacement. Captain Noakes gave the division a Dodge chassis and after a public appeal an ambulance body was fitted at a cost of £298. The Division acquired the Rolls Royce ambulance pictured above in about 1940. The 40hp Phantom 11 came from a gentleman from South Wales and was converted into an ambulance by Herbert Lomas Ltd, coachbuilders, from Manchester. Mr Leslie Doughty, who worked at the Southern Counties Garage and the father of Mrs Greener, who donated this photograph, was one of those who drove this ambulance during the war.

29. Springate Hall, the Southwick St. John Ambulance Division's Headquarters in Watling Lane was built by members of the division in their spare time. Building work started in 1938 and was finished in 1941. The duty room and ambulance garage were not on this site, but a little way away in Albion Street, overlooking Shoreham harbour.

30. Haywards Heath ARP first aid party at drill at in the early part of the war.

31. Bognor Regis Urban District Council's Austin Big 6 ambulance and an ARP Rescue Squad lorry at a bombed house in Sudley Road, Bognor Regis, August 14th 1942.

32. A Worthing ARP wartime auxiliary ambulance and attendants

33. The Aldingbourne Civil Defence unit with their auxiliary ambulance and rescue tender circa 1942. Note that the name above the door to the village hall has been painted out to confuse any enemy invaders!

34. Southwick ARP auxiliary ambulance converted from a Daimler motor car circa 1943.
Members of the Southwick St. John Division manned the ARP ambulances and local First Aid Posts throughout the war.

35. The dedication ceremony for the Henfield and District Ambulance Club's first purpose built ambulance, an Austin, on October 4[th]1944. Paid for by public subscription, it was manned by volunteers from the St. John Ambulance Brigade. Ambulance Club members had free use of the ambulance, while others had to pay according to a scale of charges.

36. Sussex 47 members and Bognor Town Council's Austin ambulance taking part in the 1945 VE Day parade along the Bognor Esplanade.

37. Pictured in October 1946, this re-bodied ex WD Bedford K Series was the newly formed Bognor St. John Division's first ambulance The vehicle remained in service until 1952.

The ambulances of the Bognor Regis Urban District Council cover, by arrangement, fifteen parishes of the Rural district, in respect of which an annual retaining fee of £75 is paid by the Rural District Council, plus a charge of 1/- per mile for all journeys undertaken. The mileage costs are recovered where possible from the users, but in necessitous cases these charges are borne by the R D C.

The Ambulance Services of the Bognor Regis Urban District Council and the St John Ambulance Brigade (Chichester Division) were supplemented during the year by the inauguration of a Hospital Car Service under which a number of private cars are available for the conveyance of persons to a hospital or other institution, whose condition does not warrant the use of a stretcher or ambulance. The service was fairly extensively used during the later part of the year, and is proving of great value to persons of limited means who are required to attend local hospitals for out-patient treatment etc.

The following statement shows the ambulance services available at the 31st December, 1945, together with details of journeys undertaken during the year.

Name of service	Area covered	Maternity Cases	Accident Cases	Cases Of General Sickness	Total Cases	Total Mileage incurred
Bognor Regis Urban District Council	Parishes of Aldingbourne, Barnham, Bersted, Eastergate, Middleton-on-Sea, Pagham, Yapton, Ford, Climping, Tortington, Walberton, Eartham, Oving, Tangmere, and NorthMundham.	13	8	101	122	2030
British Red Cross Society Detachment 63 Barnham	No defined area but principally the parishes of Aldingbourne, Barnham, Eastergate, Slindon, Walberton and Yapton.	8		63	68	1483
Chichester Division St John Ambulance	Whole Rural District except parishes covered by Bognor Regis UDC,		25	556	581	5500 (est)
British Red Cross Society, Arundel Detachment Sussex41	No defined area but principally the parishes of Eastergate, Slindon, Walberton, Tortington and Yapton.		1	8	9	187

Extract from the County Medical Officer of Health's Annual Report for 1945

38. Bognor Red Cross Detachment outside their headquarters in 1947. The building stood in the grounds of the Bognor War Memorial Hospital, exactly where the current ambulance station in Chichester Road stands today. It was moved by crane about 30 yards to the west in 1964 to make way for the new County Council built ambulance station, opened in 1966, which was itself demolished to make way for the current building in 1998.

39. The Steyning, Bramber & Beeding ambulance outside St Andrews Church, Steyning, July 8th 1947. The vehicle had been converted from a pre-war Daimler saloon car.

40. The Horsham St. John Cadet Team, winners of the 1947 National Cadet First Aid Competition held at Central Hall, Westminster.

L/R Gordon Chatfield, Gerald Jacobs, Pat Weeks, Roy Christian and Bob Myson.

The officer standing at the back is George Denyer.

41. The Dedication service for the Chichester St.John Division's new ambulance, a re-bodied ex WD Austin, in the grounds of the Bishops Palace, circa 1948

At the end of 1947 and in the run up to the commencement of the National Health Service on July 5th 1948, certain services developed rapidly.

The County is described as being "adequately served in the matter of ambulances". The St.John Ambulance Brigade had a fleet of 39 vehicles based on 10 centres (Bognor Regis, Chichester, Crawley, Henfield, Horsham, Littlehampton, Pulborough, Steyning, Southwick and Worthing) and the British Red Cross Society maintained ambulances at Arundel and Aldingbourne, and at Midhurst and Bognor Regis provided staff for vehicles owned by local authorities.

Part of Chanctonbury Rural District was served by an ambulance owned by the Storrington District Voluntary Ambulance Association and the Petworth area was served by a vehicle owned by Petworth Rural District Council. A "Hospital Car Service" for sitting cases attending out-patient departments of hospitals etc., was organised by the Women's Voluntary Service.

On the recommendation of the Ministry of Health, the practice of confining the use of certain ambulance vehicles to the removal of infectious cases was discontinued, but it was envisaged that such cases would only be dealt with by the four main stations at Bognor Regis, Chichester, Horsham and Worthing, where adequate disinfection facilities would be available.

A voluntary car service scheme was organised by the St.John Ambulance Brigade, except in Bognor Regis where the Urban District Council operated their own scheme. Hospitals using the service paid for it at a rate of 3 pence per mile.

Extract from a West Sussex County Council report published in 1947 entitled 'Now Another Pharaoh', on the transfer of responsibilities regarding the impending introduction of the National Health Service in 1948.

42. Men's Division, Chichester St.John Ambulance Brigade in the late 1940's.

The Agency Years

Section 27 of the National Health Service Act 1946 made local authorities responsible for the provision of ambulance services in their respective areas. They were authorised to do this either by direct service or 'by making arrangements with voluntary organisations or other persons for the provision by them of such ambulances, transport and staff'.

West Sussex County Council elected to take the later course, and delegated the responsibility for the provision of the service to the voluntary aid organisations, an arrangement that continued until 1963. In effect this meant little change as far as the general public were concerned, as the voluntary organisations simply continued to do what they had been doing previously. The major change was in the funding arrangements, with the County Council now responsible for funding the service.

The County's Chief Medical Officer of Health, under the County Health Department, administered the service in West Sussex.

The council took over the voluntary bodies ambulances, for which they paid them a sum of £12,000, and paid rent for their garaging. Full-time, paid ambulance drivers were provided by the St.John Ambulance Brigade - with the exception of the Midhurst areas, where the British Red Cross Society ran the service until 1961 when the County Council took over, two years before they took over from the St.John in the rest of the county. Day to day operations were controlled locally under the direction of, in the case of the St.John Divisions, their county officer, Mr George Wheatland. Volunteers continued to help man the ambulances, although as time progressed, more and more full time paid staff were employed as demands on the service increased.

Radio control of the ambulances was first introduced in the Bognor Regis and Chichester area in 1957, the system being extended to both the Worthing and Horsham districts within the next few years. The use of mobile radio sets in the ambulances meant that crews no longer had to telephone their respective controls after each journey, and that they could be quickly dispatched to any emergency that arose while they were on the road.

43. Mobile radio sets were first fitted to the county's ambulances in the Chichester area in 1957. The picture shows Doug Arthur in the cab of one of Chichester St. John Ambulance Division's Bedfords.

44. Although still a part of East Sussex at the time, this is the East Grinstead Red Cross Detachment's ambulance at the town's Queen Victoria Hospital in July 1948.
It's an Austin 'Big 6' with bodywork by Thomas Startin,

45. When the St.John Ambulance Brigade were contracted to provide the ambulance service in the Henfield area by the County Council in 1948, the Henfield Ambulance Club decided to close and their ambulance was handed over to the St.John. The vehicle was eventually transferred to Worthing in 1963 when the County Council took over direct running of the ambulance service and the ambulance station in Henfield was closed. The photo shows Members of both the Ambulance Club and the Henfield St.John Ambulance Division with the Austin ambulance at the handing over ceremony in May 1948.

46. The Sussex St.John Ambulance Brigade Band leading a procession along East Street, Chichester, circa 1950.

47. Bognor's St .John Ambulance Brigade members on parade with their ambulance fleet in the early 1950's. The vehicles are Bedfords and, far right, an Austin Welfarer. The location is the forecourt of W. Jones Garage in Lennox Street, directly opposite the unit's headquarters in Belmont Street.

48. US 7251 parked at the Chichester St.John Division's Headquarters in Coombes Yard, The Hornet, in the early 1950's. It looks like an ex wartime Civil Defence ambulance converted locally from a car, very possibly a 1930's Riley 12.

49. A new Bedford K Series ambulance with Barker & Co bodywork parked outside the Bognor St.John Divisions headquarters in Belmont Street, 1953.

50. The Horsham St.John Division's new Barker bodied Daimler DC27 ambulance at its service of dedication in Horsham Park, May 30th 1953.

51. This 1954 Bedford CA ambulance was operated by the Chichester St.John Division and had bodywork by Martin Walker Ltd of Folkstone, Kent.

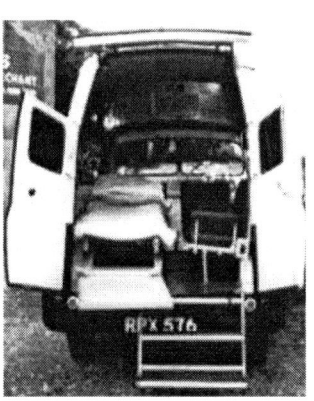

52. This style of body with its raised roof allowed enough headroom for the attendant to be able to stand up in the back.

AMBULANCES TRAVEL FARTHER THAN EVER

Despite a check on the administration of the system, the total mileage run by West Sussex County Council ambulances and hospital car services rose higher than ever before during 1951. Together the two services covered more than a million miles – ambulances a total of 313,174 miles and the car service 831,932 miles.

These figures compare with the total for ambulance services of 303,102 miles in 1950, and 269,904 miles in 1949, and for the hospital car service of 738,717 miles in 1950 and 580,560miles in 1949.

The four St.John ambulances in Worthing carried the highest number of cases - 3,701 – and they covered a total of 61,808 miles.

The two ambulances at Southwick carried 1,672 patients a total of 29,348 miles, and the ambulance at Steyning covered 3,478 miles to carry 154 patients.

Figures for the first quarter of 1952 show that there are reductions in both services on the average monthly figures for 1951, which were 26,098 miles for ambulances and 69,328 for cars. From February to March inclusive this year the monthly average for ambulances was 25,962 and for cars 67,851.

The St.John Ambulance Brigade receives a yearly grant of £17,500 from the County Council to cover the cost of its ambulance service, but this year its accounts showed an expenditure of £2,053 in excess of the grant. On request for the payment of the deficit and for the increase in the annual grant to £21,900 in view of a recent wage award and the rising cost of repair and petrol, the committee agreed to an immediate payment of £1,500 towards the 1951 deficit. Consideration of the remainder of the deficit and increasing the grant is to be given after a detailed examination of the Brigades books for each ambulance station is made by the County Treasurer.

Since suggestions by the District Auditor on the car service accounts, all abortive journeys are to be investigated and other steps are to be taken to increase efficiency.

Worthing Herald, 16th August 1952.

53. Pictured here in 1954, Horace William Parsons, or Bill as he was always known, first drove an ambulance when he joined the town's civil defence unit during the Second World War. He later became the driver of a St.John ambulance stationed in Petworth and stayed in the post until the station was closed when the County Council took over the running of the service. He then transferred to the new county service and moved to Pulborough ambulance station.

Pictured with Bill is Mrs Jones, one of a number of nurses who also manned the ambulance with him. Bill worked from his home address, day or night, and would run over to the ambulance garage to pick up the vehicle when a call came in, while his wife phoned ahead to alert the duty nurse while he was on his way over to collect her.

54. Waiting for a call-out on a sunny Sunday morning in 1956, Chichester St.John duty crews relax in the sunshine outside their headquarters in Coombes Yard in The Hornet.

55. Mr Pearce, the Commandant of Sussex 41, pictured in Arundel Park on April 28th 1956 with his Arundel Red Cross Detachment's Austin ambulance. It was purchased new in 1937 for £500 and paid for by public appeal in conjunction with the West Sussex Gazette. It had a wood panelled coach built interior with a full length fold down leather seat on the offside and metal runners to take a stretcher on the nearside. If required. a folding stretcher could be located over the lowered seat backrest to take a second stretcher case.

56. All four of Chichester St John's ambulances in Combes yard, 1956. L/R Rolls Royce, Bedford CA, Austin Sheerline and right, a Bedford K series.

57. Chicam Base. Ambulance Officer Oscar Lake manning the newly installed radio system in the Chichester St.John HQ in Coombes Yard, 1957.

58. Worthing St.John members on duty at a motorcycle grass track event in the late 1950's. The ambulance is an Austin Welfarer.

59. Southwick based Bedford J1 ambulance at Worthing hospital in the late 1950's.

60. Chichester St.John Division's new headquarters in The Hornet. Formerly D Rowe & Co's car showroom, the newly converted building was opened on April 11th 1958.

61. Alan Burbridge operating the radio equipment in the newly opened control room. Call sign Chicam Base, this control covered all the Bognor Regis, Chichester and Midhurst based ambulances.

62. Relaxing in the crew room at the new headquarters

63. A Littlehampton St.John Ambulance Brigade crew in the late 1950's loading a patient into their Bedford CA ambulance in South Terrace. Norman Oakley, at the tail of the stretcher, later became the Station Officer at Littlehampton.

64. Worthing St.John Superintendent W. H. Virgoe operating the recently installed Pye radio equipment in 'Candia', the Worthing Division's Headquarters in Farnscombe Road, February 1959. The Worthing area was the second to be equipped with this equipment following successful trials in the Bognor/Chichester area.

1960 County Councils Medical Officer of Health's report 'Health of the County', Part V – Ambulance Service

The day to day operation of the ambulance service continued to be undertaken by the St.John Ambulance Brigade on an agency basis, except in Midhurst, where the British Red Cross Society operated on the same basis. Whole-time paid staff were employed but voluntary members of the two bodies mentioned manned the ambulances at night and at weekends. There was evidence that the amount of voluntary help available for ambulance duty was not sufficient in many parts of the county.

Ambulance Stations	No of Ambulances	Accidents or emergencies	Invalids	Infectious	Total	Mileage
Bognor Regis and Chichester	7*	810	7,620	85	8,515	119,348
Crawley	4	319	4,562	-	4,881	79,596
Henfield	1	83	558	-	641	15,030
Horsham	3	345	1,538	25	1,908	46,063
Littlehampton	2	291	2,208	-	2,499	41,741
Midhurst	1	62	783	-	845	19,730
Petworth	1	112	576	-	688	18,134
Pulborough	1	98	696	-	794	21,619
Southwick	2	229	3,250	-	3,479	43,946
Worthing	5	758	9.075	104	9,937	80,630
Totals	27	3,107	30,866	214	34,187	485,837

- Including "spare" to be used wherever required.

65. In the late 1950's this Petworth based St.John Ambulance Brigade Bedford J Type was garaged next to the Council Offices at the junction of Station Road, Midhurst Road and Pound Street. A slot had to be cut out above the garage door to give clearance for a roof mounted blue beacon when it was fitted a few years later! The driver in his summer issue uniform jacket is Bill Parsons.

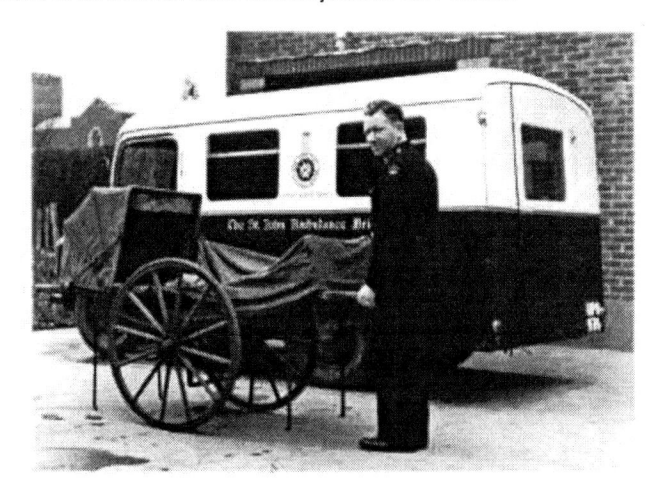

66. The 1960s photograph shows Norman Oakley (who later went on to become the Station Officer at Littlehampton Ambulance Station) with the town's original 1911 Ashford Litter. The stretcher bed could be removed from the wheeled carriage and a canvas hood and modesty apron could be fitted as shown. The folding legs would be raised during transport. The ambulance is a Bedford CA.

AMBULANCE TAKE-OVER BY COUNTY APPROVED

The County Council on Friday approved its Health Committees recommendation which means, in effect, that ambulance and hospital car services will be operated directly by the county Council from April 1st 1963.

Before the meeting the entrance to County Hall was picketed by members of the Chichester Division of the St.John Ambulance Brigade, bearing placards protesting at the proposal. There was no disturbance, and the 12 pickets entered the public gallery to hear the debate.

The Health Committee's recommendation was carried after a 53-35 vote in favour.

Agency Agreement

Ald. E.G.Harvey, Chairman of the County Health Committee, introducing the proposal said "The responsibility for providing this important service has, since 1948, been that of the County Council, and to do that the responsibility has been discharged by an agency agreement with the St.John Ambulance Brigade and the British Red Cross Society."

"The cost of the service, when the agency started, was £30,000 the first year. This year it will be in excess of £100, 000, and is likely to increase if certain recommendations are approved. The Health Committee discussed it fully and with one exception were of the opinion that the service ought to come under the control of the County. If this were done fewer vehicles and staff would be required."

He went on to say "There are only three other counties in the country who relied on an agency agreement as in West Sussex."

Misunderstanding

Ald Harvey said that there seemed to be some misunderstanding amongst ambulance personnel that the County Council would not require any voluntary service if it took over the administration of the service.

"Of course voluntary service will be required ..... I would like to assure all those interested that the council, through the ambulance service, will ensure that opportunity for voluntary service will continue," said Ald. Harvey. He also expressed appreciation for the service given in the past by the Brigade

Ald. The Duke of Norfolk said that the voluntary services of this country were held in the highest regard, and that any form of interference with them went against the grain. But Ald Harvey made a very fair statement.

"If it so happens in the next 18 months, before this comes into operation, there is any sign that expenditure goes up and not down, I shall oppose it most strongly." he said.

Coun. Mrs D. Stapleton Skinner said that she feared that if the County took over the service voluntary workers would lose the important jobs and would resign. She had opposed the idea when it was considered by the Health Committee.

Coun. Lady Prior-Palmer O.B.E. said that it was difficult for anyone outside the Health Committee to form an opinion on the matter, but it was clear that there must be some changes in the ambulance service.

"On the other hand, it seems that this recommendation is premature. I think there should be more discussion between the Brigade and the Council before we come to a decision." she said.

Ald. Harvey replying said that discussions had taken place between the county and the Brigade for several months. The suggestion by Coun. Mrs.Sapleton Skinner that the Brigade would die if the county took over the service was "surely, ridiculous."

Extract from the Worthing Herald, 1st December 1961.

67. Southwick St.John's Bedford J Type Ambulance at the Queen Victoria Hospital in East Grinstead in the early 1960's. This vehicles call sign was Worham Grey.

68. An Austin Sheerline Ambulance belonging to the Littlehampton St. John Division in the early 1960's.

69. Haywards Heath Ambulance Station in 1961 with a Bedford J Type Ambulance in the garage.

70. Chichester St. John Division's Bedford J type in the early 1960's.

71. In 1961 the Southwick St.John Ambulance Division purchased two ambulances in order to provide a non NHS service for private patients and nursing homes. In 1963 the charge for private journeys was 2/6d per mile. This pre-war Humber ambulance was purchased from a Surrey St.John Division for £85, and completely renovated before being put back into service.

72. This is the second of these vehicles, an ex Civil Defence Ford.

74. A Bedford J1 ambulance manned by members of the Midhurst Red Cross. The centre provided the ambulance service in the Midhurst area under the County Council Agency Agreement until 1961, when the County Council took over the service, two years before it did so in the rest of the county.

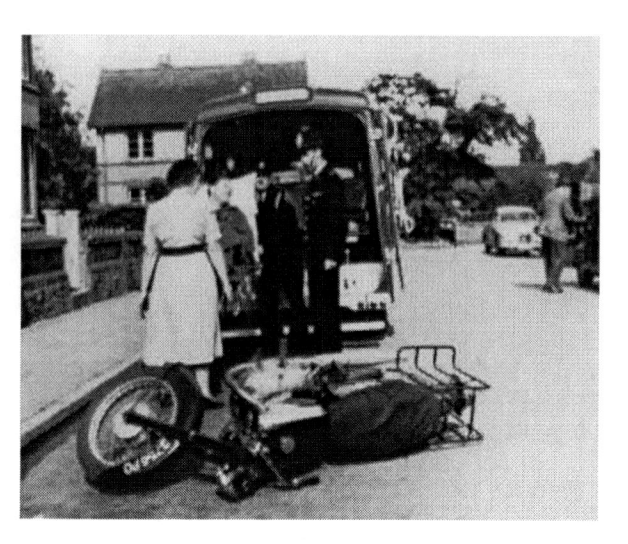

75. Worthing St.John Ambulance Brigade's Daimler DC27 ambulance. The crew are preparing to take part in a carnival procession in the early 1960s.

VIEWPOINT
Change

It is sad to think that soon the familiar insignia of the St.John Ambulance Brigade will be missing from the sides of our ambulances, where it has been proudly displayed for almost fifty years. The fact remains that in April West Sussex County Council is taking over the hospital ambulance service and instead of the familiar black and white vehicles we will have them in cream and blue and minus the St.John badge.

These are the only outward signs the public will see of the changeover, for the county will naturally see to it that the same high standards of service is maintained.

But it marks the end of an era and we know that we are not alone in being sad at it's departure. Indeed we are not convinced that the change was absolutely necessary.

The St John ambulance Brigade takes immense pride in the service it renders. Full-time drivers are naturally paid but they owe their allegiance to a voluntary organisation which has gained wonderful prestige over the years. The esprit de corps is second to none. In addition they have been backed up by part-time workers in the same great organisation.

Now this spirit is to be thrown overboard and will be one that has to be built up from scratch. It is strangely odd that in this Welfare State of ours the efforts of voluntary organisations who want to serve the community are gradually being whittled away. How many years will it take for the spirit of voluntary community service to disappear altogether?

Extract from the Worthing Gazette, September 5th 1962

75. Chichester St.John Ambulance Brigade's new fleet of vehicles parked outside Barford House in 1963. They were bought to replace their old fleet that was transferring to the County Council run service. The Bedford to the right hand side of the photograph is an ex Civil Defence rescue vehicle.

76. The newly opened headquarters building of the Southwick Division of the St.John Ambulance Brigade in 1963, who, at the time this photograph was taken, were still providing the ambulance service for the area under the County Councils agency agreement. This new building in the Twitten replaced their earlier headquarters in Watling Lane.

The £12,000 needed to build the new headquarters was raised by public donation and a loan of £3,000 from the Order of St.John. It contained a three bay ambulance garage, a duty room complete with kitchen and toilet, a recreation room and a large hall for training and social events.

West Sussex County Councils annual report 'The Health of The County' states that the four ambulances and 5 staff at Southwick conveyed a total of 5,935 patients and travelled 43,257 miles in the process.

The County Council had hoped to use this building for their directly controlled service which was due to come into operation on April 1st 1963, but unfortunately a disagreement over rent prevented this from happening, and consequently a new ambulance station was built off Stoney Lane in Shoreham instead.

77. Southwick's Superintendent Arthur Bunch doing some running repairs to one of the Division's older ambulances.

46

The County Council Era 1963 - 1974

In 1961, after undertaking a prolonged review of the costs and efficiencies of providing ambulances services within the county, West Sussex County Council decided to end the existing agency arrangements and bring the provision of the service under it's direct control. Letters informing the voluntary societies that the current arrangements were to end on the 31st March 1963 were sent out by the Clerk of the Council in July 1962.

Likewise, East Sussex County Council took over the service from the Red Cross at Haywards Heath and East Grinstead in 1966, opening a brand new ambulance station in Burgess Hill in1969.

According to a November 1961 report in the Worthing Herald, the reasons for ending the agency arrangements included the increase in the county's population from 312,700 in 1959 to 411, 000 at the 1961 census, the increasing costs of the provision, rising from £32.000 in 1949/50 to an estimated £102,000 for the current year (1961), and the difficulty some voluntary organisations had in maintaining a sufficient number of volunteers to supplement the small number of full time paid staff.

However the St.John County Commissioner had stated that the Brigade did wish to continue with the old arrangements and that it would be a sad day if they were to come to an end, but if and when they did the Brigade would continue to offer its support to the new service. Indeed many St. John members continued to volunteer for duty with the new county service until the practice came to an end in 1972 when the service became wholly full time.

It was also appreciated by the council that, with the county's population levels continuing to rise, it was unrealistic to expect the requirements of the both public and the local medical professionals to be met by a service that was at times stretched by lack of available resources.

With the forthcoming changes in mind, the council appointed Mr V A Glover to the post of County Ambulance Officer in September 1961. Based at County Hall under the direction of the County's Ambulance Sub-Committee and the County Medical Officer, he oversaw the transition and became responsible for the day to day operation of the service and for planning its future development.

A ceremony to mark the changeover to the new service took place in bright sunshine at County Hall on Sunday March 27th. Members of the St.John Ambulance Brigade, the British Red Cross Society and of the new West Sussex County Council Ambulance Service paraded in front of the Duchess of Norfolk, County President of the Red Cross Society, Lord Rupert Neville, County President of the St.John Ambulance Brigade and officers of the County Council. A Service of Dedication was led by the Archdeacon of Chichester, the Venerable Lancelot Mason.

The existing ambulance stations were owned by the county's St.John Divisions, who not unnaturally, wished to retain these for there own use. Therefore new ambulance stations had to be designed and built and arrangements made for the temporary accommodation of crews and vehicles until they were ready. Crews at Bognor were housed on the top floor of a council owned care home in Hawthorn Road, complete with external metal staircase, while Littlehampton crews moved into a room above the town's mortuary!

78. The ceremony held at County Hall, Chichester on Sunday 27th March 1963 to mark the changeover to the council run ambulance service.

Even though the council found some difficulty in locating suitable land in many towns, the building programme progressed steadily, with the first of the new stations, Crawley, opening in December 1961, followed by Midhurst in 1963. The plans for an ambulance station in the Witterings area were dropped in 1965. All of the remaining ambulance stations were in use by1968.

Initially not all the stations were open for 24hrs a day, many working a 'stand by' system with the driver taking the vehicle home with him at the end of a day and collecting the attendant en-route to a call.

The County Council, who had funded the purchase of all the county's ambulances under the agency agreement of 1948, were the legal owners of the vehicles, and they were handed back to the county's control in 1963. They retained their existing St John colour scheme of black and white, but had a blue stripe applied to the sides that bore West Sussex County Council lettering. All the new ambulances the council purchased from then on were finished in an all-over cream livery and carried the county badge as well. The council's annual report of 1963 lists the ambulance fleet at 34 vehicles with a total of 67 whole time ambulance men.

Training standards continued to improve during this period. A Staff Officer responsible for training was appointed in 1965 and induction programs for new recruits introduced. A Cadet Scheme was inaugurated the same year and three 17year olds began a three year long course during which, as well as attending colleges of further education, they received training in casualty and other hospital departments, in ambulance control and at various ambulance stations.

By the end of 1972 the service had 6 nationally qualified instructors, and new staff attended a two week induction course where they were taught basic first aid and operating procedures, followed as soon as possible by a six week residential course at a regional training school. Driver training, command and control and supervisory courses were also available, and all staff were required to attend two week long refresher courses on a regular basis.

79. The old & the new style uniforms, County Council on the left and St John on the right
From an old newspaper cutting

80. 'The Hut', the temporary accommodation provided for Chichester crews located in the grounds of County Hall Chichester. It also contained a continuously manned central control, which dealt with all the counties 999 calls and all the non-urgent calls usually covered by the area controls in Horsham and Worthing between 6pm and 8am and at weekends. 1963 also saw the beginnings of 'out-posting' of radio controlled ambulances at peak load periods

81. In 1963 Littlehampton crews were based in the old mortuary building at Littlehampton Hospital until their new station was opened in East Street in 1967.

82. Horsham based Morris LD ambulance, reg no 676 CPX, soon after the County Council took the vehicle over from the town's St John Ambulance Division, whose livery it still carries, augmented with the County Council's blue side stripe and lettering.

A feature of the early days of the County Council operated service were the Ambulance Proficiency Competitions. In 1963 Pat Weeks (Horsham) and Chub Weston (Crawley) won both the regional and the national competitions at their first attempt. They beat an initial entry of 61 teams from across the country to get to the national finals and then beat the other six finalists at Morton-in-the-Marsh to win the team test, best attendant and best driver awards as well as the overall title, the first time all the trophies had ever been won by a single team.

83. Pat and Chub photographed being observed by the judges during their team test at the regional competition held in Battersea Park in 1963.

84. Pat Weeks (second from left) and Chub Weston (second from right) at County Hall, Chichester, with the Pye Rose Bowl awarded to the overall winners of the National Championships. Standing far left is County Ambulance Officer Vince Glover with, far right, Superintendent George Wheatland.

85. Worthing c1963. The town's County Council ambulances were temporarily based in this building at the rear of the St.John headquarters in Farncombe Road.

86. The first new ambulance station to be built by the County Council was in Exchange Road, Crawley, to the rear of the Police Station, and opened on 10th December 1961, two years before the council took over direct administration of the service. The two ambulances in this 1963 photograph are BMC J2's.

87. The new ambulance station at Midhurst came into use on July 10th 1963 and was officially opened on November 10th by Her Grace the Duchess of Norfolk.
Lord Newton, Parliamentary Secretary to the Minister for Health, visited the building on September 16th. The ambulance staff are, left to right, Gordon Geall, Alan Kitley, Doreen Culverston and Vic Charman.

88. Crawley Ambulance Station, 1964. A/M Goff Tame with a new Wadham bodied Morris LD ambulance.

53

89. This Bedford CA ambulance at Midhurst Ambulance Station in 1964 is still in the St John Ambulance Brigade's black and white livery, but with the addition of the County Council Badge and blue side stripe. The vehicle was sold in 1965 for £65.

90. May 30th 1964, and ambulance staff from across the County gather at County Hall, Chichester, for the start of that years Ambulance Efficiency Competition. From left to right they are: Len Riley, Jack Pitts, Cecil Tuckey, Bob Hope and Chub Weston. Ambulances from left to right are Bedford J Type, BMC J2, Bedford CA Utilicon and Wadham/Morris LD.

91. The St.John building behind the village hall in Pulborough was used by County Council ambulance crews until the new ambulance station in Moat Road was opened in 1966. The ambulance is an LD 111.

92. Ambulanceman Brian Knight with Midhurst's new Austin Gypsy 4x4 ambulance in 1964.

Station	Staff	Vehicles	Mileage	Patients
Bognor Regis	9	6	103,060	26,110
Chichester	16	6	101,349	16,132
Crawley	10	6	98,574	15,487
Horsham	11	4	81,828	9,445
Littlehampton	5	2	59,978	5,153
Midhurst	4	2	50,784	3,771
Pulborough	2	2	38,707	1,224
Shoreham	5*	2	48,485	6,923
Worthing	21*	8	145,939	26,270
Totals	83	38	728,704	110,515

* Includes both full and part time staff.

The counties ambulance statistics for 1965

93. The counties ambulance officers in 1966.
Back row L/R Bill Parsons, Harry Shurety, Vic Charman, Stan Linsted, Bill Mills, Allan Ware, Sid Lacey, Harry Burton, Ted Ayres.
Front row L/R Wilf Virgo, Doug Arthur, Graham Tilley, County Ambulance Officer Mr. Vince Glover, Pat Weeks, Oscar Lake, George Wheatland.

New Ambulance Stations

West Sussex County Council's ambulance station building program continued during the mid 1960's, using the same SCOLA (Second Consortium of Local Authorities) pre-fabricated steel frame construction method used to build many other local authority buildings of the period, such as schools and libraries.
All the new stations were completed by 1968.

94. Worthing, opened in 1966.

95. Pulborough, opened in 1966.

96. Shoreham, opened in 1966.

97. Chichester, opened in 1966.

98. Bognor Regis, opened in 1966.

99. Littlehampton opened in 1967.

100. Horsham, opened in 1968.

101. Wadham /Morris LD ambulance at Midhurst Ambulance Station circa1966

102. Wadham bodied BMC J2 at Worthing Ambulance Station c1966.

103. Worthing based Wadham BMC JU250 ambulance circa 1967.

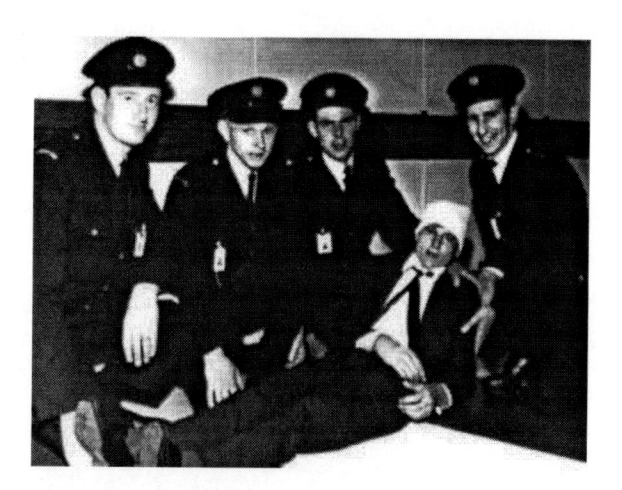

104. Seven teams entered the county's 1969 Ambulance Efficiency Competition held In Chichester in May. The victors were this team from Chichester Ambulance Station.
L/R Brian Attfield, Alan Hurst, Trevor Roman and Allan Ware. The team went on to take 6th place in the Regional Finals in June.

105. East Sussex County Council ended its agency agreement with the Red Cross in 1966 and set up its own directly administered service. Opened in 1969, this is the East Sussex County Council built ambulance station in East Court, Burgess Hill, in 1970. All the ambulances are Bedford J1's, the one on the left is still in it's old Red Cross livery while one second from right has the more modern looking bodywork by Marshals of Cambridge.

106. Officers and staff at Crawley Ambulance Station in 1971.

107. The ambulances lined up outside Worthing Ambulance Station, in August 1972 are a mixture of Ford Transits, Morris LD's and BMC Ju250's.

108. Worthing ambulance staff, August 1972

109. Haywards Heath ambulancemen Peter Woller and Barry Tiller (left) with the Lomas Shield won at the 1972 Regional finals of the National Efficiency tests held at the Downs Secondary School in Newhaven. A second team from Haywards Heath consisting of John Mercer and Chris Rose also took part in that year's event.

Stations	Staff	Vehicles
Ambulance Control	18	
Bognor Regis	10*	6
Chichester	20*	9
Crawley	20*	10
Horsham	9	4
Littlehampton	5	2
Midhurst	4	2
Pulborough	4	2
Shoreham	5	2
Worthing	33	12
Totals	128	49

- Includes both full and part time staff.

Ambulance service statistics for 1972

110. Bognor Ambulance Station staff in 1973. L/R back row: Kieth Merryman, Mick Airey, Dennis Croucher, Vince Shaw, Tim Murgatroyd, Roger Farley, Dennis Highfield. L/R front row; Roy Tharle, Brian Knight, Station Officer Peter Wells, Peggy Newman, Andy Brian.

111. Opened in 1973, the new Ambulance Control in Summersdale Road, Chichester, replaced the existing one located in the adjacent ambulance station.

112. Crawley's new ambulance station in Ifield Avenue, opened in 1973.

113. Amongst the vehicles lined up on the lawn of the Bognor Regis War Memorial Hospital ready for the hospitals 1973 fete are Wadham/Morris LD'111's, BMC JU250's, Ford Transits and Land Rovers. Far left, with its bonnet up, is a guest London Ambulance Service Daimler DC27.

65

West Sussex Area Heath Authority 1974 – 1982

Two events were to change the face of the county's ambulance service yet again in the mid 1970's. The first was the implementation of the National Health Service Reorganisation Act of 1973, which transferred the responsibility for the provision of the ambulance service from the county councils to the National Health Service. The second was the report by the Commission on Local Government that re-drew West Sussex's county boundary, incorporating within it areas formally parts of Surrey and East Sussex.

West Sussex Area Health Authority, with its headquarters at Courtlands in Worthing, took over the ambulance service on April 1st 1974, and Pat Weeks was appointed as the new services Chief Ambulance Officer. Once again the County's Ambulance Service had new masters.

As a result of the boundary changes the towns of East Grinstead, Haywards Heath and Burgess Hill became part of West Sussex, and their ambulance staff and premises were transferred to the new authority. Gatwick Airport, formally in Surrey, now lay in West Sussex, but the ambulance station serving it remained just north of the new boundary, so for geographical and political reasons Surrey Ambulance Service continued to provide cover for the airport in exchange for reciprocal arrangements elsewhere.

The new service inherited a total of 167 staff and 62 vehicles from the two County Council services. The ambulance livery changed from a blue to an orange coloured stripe on the side of the vehicles along with the lettering West Sussex Area Health Authority, although some of the older vehicles continued to carry the old County Council badge.

There were initially two operational divisions; Alpha Division, under Superintendent David Hook, who was based at Chichester Ambulance Station and comprising Bognor Regis, Chichester, Horsham, Littlehampton, Midhurst and Pulborough ambulance stations and Bravo Division under Superintendent A. (Chub) Weston, based at Burgess Hill, comprising Burgess Hill, Crawley, East Grinstead, Haywards Heath, Shoreham, and Worthing ambulance stations.

In 1977 this changed to three Divisions, A Division comprising Chichester, Bognor and Midhurst ambulance stations with Superintendent Allan Ware in charge, B Division with Superintendent Weston in charge and consisting of Crawley, Burgess Hill, East Grinstead, Haywards Heath and Horsham ambulance stations and finally C Division under Superintendent Bob Jefferies consisting of Worthing, Shoreham, Pulborough and Littlehampton ambulance stations.

West Sussex Area Health Authority Ambulance Service

The present service became directly operated on 1st April 1974, prior to which it was operated by the west Sussex County Council. Since the inception of the National Health service in 1948 the service was operated on an agency basis by the British Red Cross Society and the St John Ambulance Brigade. The co-ordination of the various elements presented many problems, but it was realised that the dominating factor governing the administration and operation of the ambulance service must be the needs of the patients for whom the service was to be provided.

Since 1963 there has been a steady growth in the work of the service, particularly in day hospital attendances, and in 1972 153,014 patients were conveyed 900.167 miles by ambulances, and 113,489 patients were conveyed 1,152,754 miles by ambulance cars. 718 patients had part of their journeys arranged by rail.

Control

The service is based on a central control in Chichester and 12 ambulance stations, all modern purpose built buildings, the total staff establishment being 167 and ambulances 62.

The movement of staff and vehicles is controlled from the central control, which is manned on a 24hr basis by 23 staff. The number of patients for whom transport is arranged is approximately 7,000 weekly. A new control became operational at the end of April 1973, and was designed from experience gained in the previous control, which was situated in what is now the ambulance station and training centre. In addition to the work of the ambulances, an ambulance car service with approximately 300 voluntary drivers is administered, and without these drivers it would be impossible to deal with the large volume of work. The car service work is steadily growing, and more car drivers are needed to cope with the increasing demand.

Vehicles

The service is standardising on Ford Transit chassis, and the ambulances are equipped with all up-to-date equipment. The vehicles are kept in a high condition of efficiency by stringent three monthly inspections, together with regular tyre checks by experts.

Training

Ambulance staff are now highly trained, all new recruits being given a short local induction course, followed within a few months by a six week course at an Area Training School. Staff in post attend the school every three years for a two week refresher course, and there are further courses available for driving and control as well as first line supervisory courses and middle management courses for officers. An in-service training syllabus is being put into operation shortly to keep staff up to date with the more important procedures. The service has six nationally trained instructors, and takes an important part in area and national training.

General

The service has had the use of computers in producing its statistics for some years, and is testing photo-facsimile equipment for passing journey details from control to ambulance stations, the first service in the country to do so.

The service suffers from the fact that it has no control over the requests received, and it is very difficult for the staff of hospital departments to appreciate those other hospital departments and general practitioners also require transport for their patients, which must be fitted in with answering the ever increasing number of emergency calls received. The public expects a high standard of service these days, and there are inevitably occasions when resources available are strained to the limit. Even one wasted journey because the patient did not require transport, or did not know it was coming, means delay in picking up other patients. Similarly, a request for transport at short notice because someone has forgotten to order it, or asking for an ambulance when the patient is able to travel by car can cause difficulty in providing transport for other patients.

Reorganisation

Reorganisation is a challenge to us all, but the ambulance service should reap benefit from having much closer links with the main users, and a more efficient service for the patients and hospitals should result.

On 1st April 1974, the new service became Area administered, the Chief Ambulance Officer being responsible to the Area Administrator for its efficient operation.

The ambulance stations at Burgess Hill, East Grinstead and Haywards Heath in East Sussex were merged with the present West Sussex Service and Gatwick in Surrey will shortly be following suit. The total establishment for staff will be approximately 230, and vehicles approximately 70. There will be a direct telephone link between the control tower switchboard at Gatwick airport and the Chichester Ambulance Control, and closer co-operation is envisaged between the West Sussex and Surrey services in the event of any major incident.

The ambulance car service will have approximately 300 cars, and with additional day hospitals scheduled to open in the next year or two, the work is expected to grow.

P.J Weeks, Chief Ambulance Officer

Report issued by the Chief Ambulance Officer in April 1974

114. Built by East Sussex County Council and opened in 1969, East Grinstead Ambulance Station was transferred to West Sussex Ambulance Service in 1974 because of county boundary changes.

115. The interior of Crawley Ambulance Station garage in 1975. On the left is an early Wadham bodied Ford Transit (fleet no 58) with a later model Hanlon bodied vehicle (fleet no 11) on the right. On the table between them is a selection of the equipment carried at the time. The older vehicle still carries the County Council badge between the saloon windows, while both now have an orange stripe along the sides instead of the County Council blue ones.

116. The crew rest room at Crawley Ambulance Station in 1975.

69

117. Pulborough based Hanlon bodied 3 litre Ford Transit, XPX 567L, call sign 66, on the seafront at Southsea circa1975.

118. The interior view of 66 showing equipment layout.

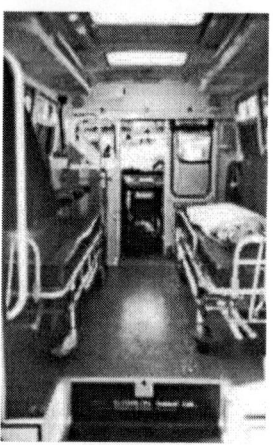

119. Worthing based Land Rover ambulance circa1975,

120. Range Rover 4x4 ambulance, call sign 23, at Chichester Ambulance Station circa 1976.

121. Ex WSCC Mk1 Ford Transit ambulance at Worthing Hospital in 1977.

71

122. Bedford J Type at Worthing Ambulance Station in 1977. These vehicles had been transferred from East Sussex Ambulance Service in 1974. At least one of these ended its service as a training vehicle on the skid pan at Goodwood airfield.

123. Crawley based incident support Land Rover c1978.

72

124. Worthing based Range Rover NNJ 270P at Pulborough Ambulance Station open Day, July 1978.

125. West Sussex Ambulance Service team, 1978 Royal Military Police March. From L/R: Front row, Pete Williams, Allan Ware, Martin Guarnaccio (holding shield). Second row, Jim Boxhall, Alan Hurst, Bill Penn. Third row, Ray Harper, Brian Janman, Ray Ballantyne. Back row, Brian Attfield, Brian Jones, Roger Saych.

126. The staff of Crawley Ambulance Station 1978.

127. Haywards Heath1980. L/R a Hanlon bodied Bedford CF, WAP 901S (287), and two Wadham bodied Bedford CFs. NAP 151P (218) and NAP 152P (219).

128. On the skid pan at Goodwood.

Driver Training in the 1980's

129. Up on the South Downs in the snow.

130. Course members with 'The Hearse'(a Ford Granada) at the old Training School at Swandean Hospital in Worthing.

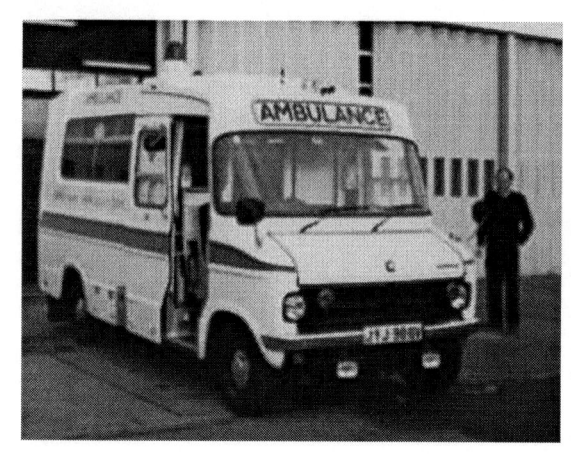

131. QAM Tim Murgatroyd and Hanlon Hi-Line Bedford CF ambulance JYJ 986W (call sign 254) on the forecourt at Bognor Regis Ambulance Station in 1980.

132. Ambulancemen from Pulborough Ambulance Station set up the charity 'Arun Cardiac Emergency' (ACE) in 1978 to raise funds for advanced life saving equipment with the support of local GP Dr Shillingford. By 1981 they were able to equip all three of the station's vehicles with defibrillators, cardiac monitoring equipment and advanced airway management kits as seen in the photo above.
L/R station Officer Keith Dellows, Dave Weir, Leading ambulanceman Alan Furminger, Phil Reid. Neil Ellis. Burt Greenfield and Bob Mitchell.

133. The Fire Service attending to Horsham's Bedford CF sitting case vehicle after an electrical fire in 1981.

134. The mobilisation desk in Ambulance Control, Summersdale Rd, Chichester, circa early 1980's

West Sussex Ambulance Service 1982 – 1995

The consultative paper 'Patients First' issued by the Secretary of State for Social Services in 1979 paved the way for the next major change in the way that health services were provided. Its aim was to eliminate one layer of administration, the Area Health Authorities, and devolve the provision of health services down to district level.

The 1980 Health Services Bill came into effect on April 1st 1982, and with the abolition of the West Sussex Area Health Authority the Chichester, Worthing and Mid Downs District Health Authorities took charge of their own affairs. As a countywide organisation the ambulance service did not fit neatly into this new scheme, so the Worthing District Health Authority undertook the management of the service on behalf of the others, with all three authorities contributing their own share of the services budget. This new service became the West Sussex Ambulance Service. At the time of formation the service had a staff of approximately 230 and operated 87 ambulances.

In 1983 the services training school moved from its old home in Chichester Ambulance Station into a more central location in what was previously the isolation ward at Swandean Hospital in Worthing. Induction, post proficiency and driver training courses were held there under the direction of Peter Wells, the services Training Officer. In 1984 front line staff began to be trained in cardiac monitoring and defibrillation, but, as funding to buy the new equipment was not available through the service itself, crews from across the county set about raising the money themselves. So successful were they that, with the help of local charities and organisations, every emergency ambulance in the county carried cardiac monitors and defibrillators within two years.

1987 saw a major change within the service when the 24hr emergency service and the routine outpatient service were separated. This meant that front line emergency crews no longer dealt with the outpatient work leaving them more freely available to respond to emergency and urgent calls, resulting in a significant improvement in response times. First tier staff now worked 12hr shifts around the clock, week-ends and bank holidays, with relief cover for holiday and sickness built into their rota.

The new Patient Transport Service, or PTS for short, now equipped with dedicated vehicles of their own, was in turn able to provide a more reliable service to the various hospital outpatient departments and day units. PTS staff worked 8hr shifts, Monday to Friday, with hour long lunch breaks built into their rota, a luxury not afforded to front line A/E crews.

Experience in other areas, most notably Brighton and Bristol, had shown the worth of training ambulance staff in advanced resuscitation techniques. The extended skills of endotracheal intubation, intravenous fluid replacement therapy and drug administration allowed crews to provide far more effective treatment for many serious medical conditions both before and during transport to hospital. In 1988 the NHS Training Authority implemented a national program to train emergency ambulance staff in these skills. The first West Sussex staff to undertake this training did so at the Regional Training School in Banstead, Surrey, West Sussex gaining accreditation to teach the course in-house in 1991.

The Badge of
THE NATIONAL HEALTH SERVICE
AMBULANCE SERVICES OF ENGLAND
AND WALES

TO BE WORN WITH PRIDE & HONOUR

The new Crown Badge was given the Royal seal of approval by Her Majesty Queen Elizabeth II and dedicated to the National Health Service Ambulance Services of England and Wales at a special service held at York Minster on September the 19th 1985,

Not Your Average Night Shift

October 12th 1984. Night shift at Midhurst Ambulance Station. All settled down and snug as usual, when, at 3.15 the red phone rang …. "Emergency call for you in Brighton". No further details were given, other than my crew mate Neville Till and I were to rendezvous with other West Sussex ambulances on the A27 Shoreham flyover, from where we would be escorted to Brighton Promenade.

We were led to the seafront and parked up opposite the Grand and Metropole Hotels. We couldn't believe the devastation before our eyes, there was a gaping great hole in the front of the Grand Hotel that reached from the roof to ground level, and the whole area was covered in dust and rubble, the result of the now infamous IRA bomb attack on the Tory Party conference.

We were detailed by the Senior Ambulance Officer on scene, Rowley Grainger, to attend to a number of casualties on the promenade and beach, some of whom had minor injuries and were shocked by their experiences. Norman Tebbit was rescued by the Fire Brigade and taken to the Royal Sussex County Hospital by ambulance while we were there. At about 04.45 it was decided that the remaining East Sussex Ambulance Service units should be withdrawn from the scene so that they could get back to dealing with local incidents and 999 calls, leaving units from Surrey, Kent and West Sussex on scene. These units began to be stood down and RTB'd at around 07.30 as fresh East Sussex crews came on duty and began to organise themselves for the clearing up tasks.

At 10.30, we were just about the last to leave the scene, having still not really taken in all we had just witnessed and dealt with. It was a night shift I will never forget.

Harry Harper

135. There has always been a strong social element in the ambulance service and for many years Chichester Ambulance Station fielded a team in their local football league.
Pictured here are the 1981-2 season's team comprising, from left to right; Back row, Clive Strudwick, Martin Guarnaccio, Ben Ayling, Brian Boxall, Steve Johnson, Alan Hurst and Adrian White. Front row, left to right, Allan Ware, Dave Phillips, Dave Arthur, Harry Harper and Bob Fenwick.

Representing The Service

136. 1984 Chichester RMP March. The team from West Sussex Ambulance Service marching along North Street, Chichester.
The standard is being carried by Divisional Officer Allan Ware.

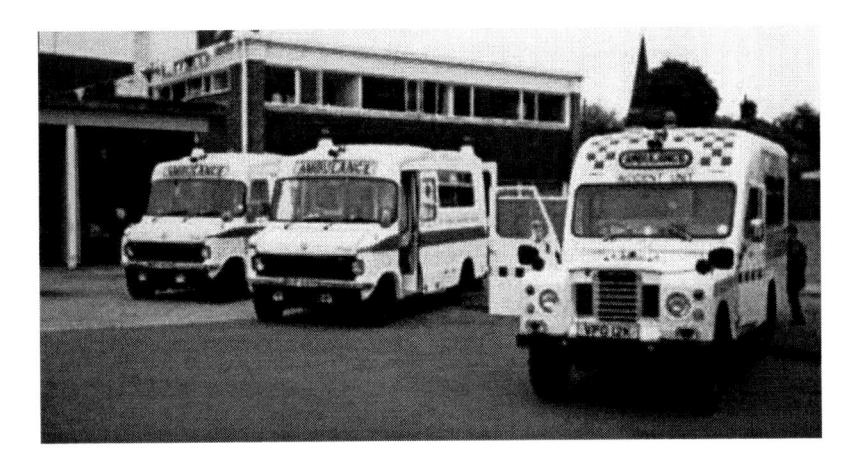

137. Burgess Hill Ambulance Station 1984 open day.

Fundraising for Charity

138. Littlehampton ambulance staff at the start of the 1985 Arun Bath Tub Race, fund raising for their cardiac equipment fund.

139. Land Rover ambulance with a major incident trailer attached, Worthing Ambulance Station, 1988.

140. Ford Transit sitting case vehicle, fleet number 125, at Bognor Regis, July 1987.

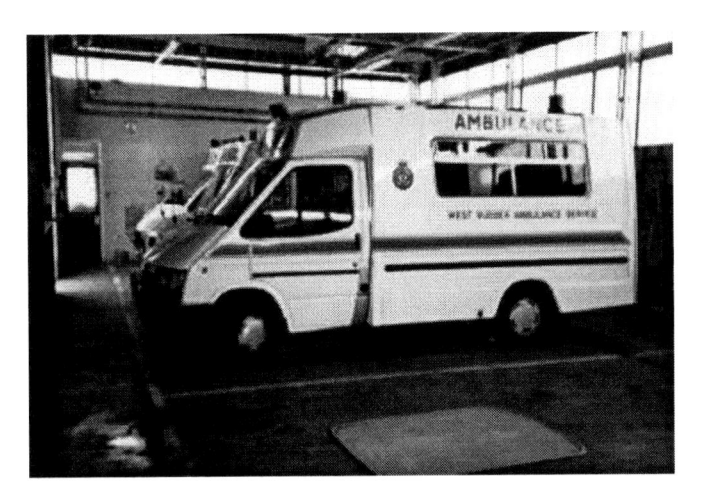

141. M.I.A.B.bodied Ford Transit front line ambulance in the garage at Bognor Ambulance Station in April 1988.

142. Originally intended for use as a PTS vehicle, and fitted with a wheelchair tail lift, this 1978 Ford A Series was found to be unsuitable for the role and was then converted into the county's mobile control unit by the staff at Ambulance Control in Chichester. With the fleet number of 321 it was inevitably nicknamed "Dusty Bin" and was sold off for preservation in 1991. It is pictured above parked behind Chichester Ambulance Control in 1988.

143. Two Hanlon bodied Ford Transits (C57 JVX, left and C299 OCD) at East Grinstead Ambulance Station in the late 1980's.

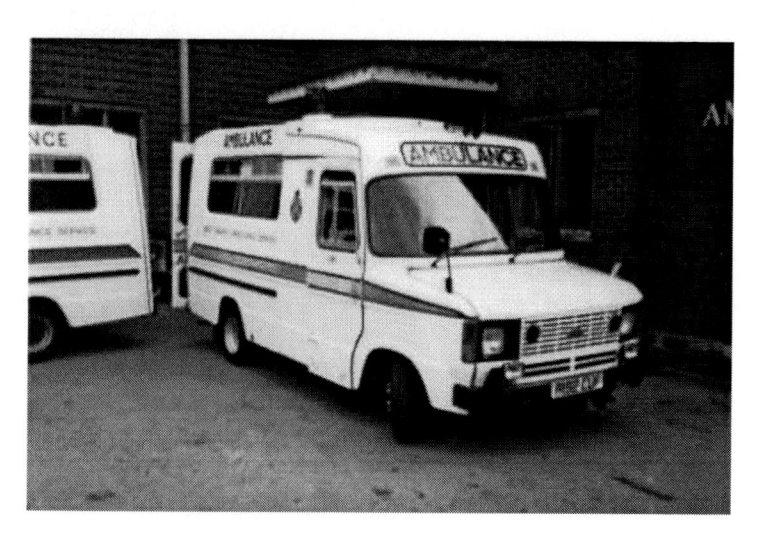

144. Bognor based Mk2 3 litre Ford Transit ambulance A192 CUF, call sign 229, at King Edward V11 Hospital, Midhurst in 1989.

145. Attending a minor road traffic accident in Worthing, March 1989.

146. Mr. Ken Smith, who had previously served in both the London and Kent Ambulance Services, was appointed to the post of Chief Ambulance Officer for West Sussex in 1989

85

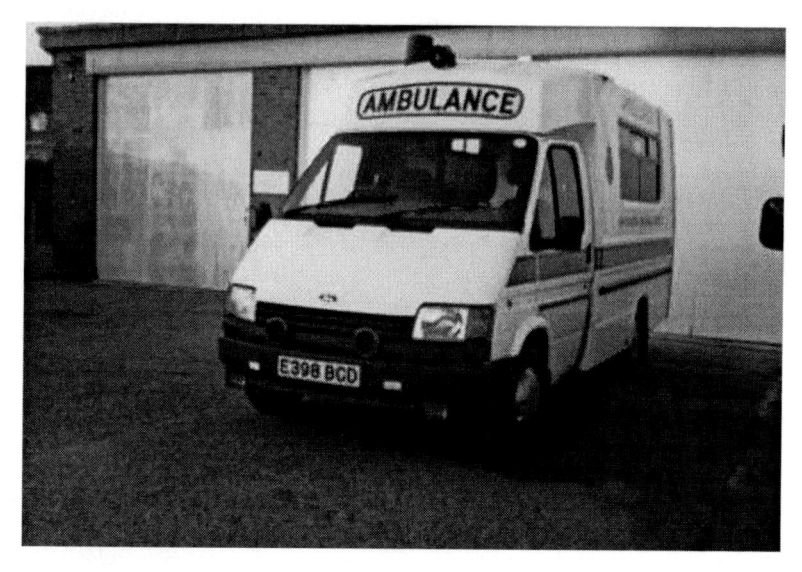

147. Wadham M.I.A.B. (Modular Interchangeable Ambulance Body) bodied Ford Transit Mk3 ambulance E398 BCD, fleet no.210, at Burgess Hill Ambulance Station in the late 1980's.

148. The newly opened ambulance station in Yeoman Road, Worthing, 1989.

149. East Grinstead Ambulance Station in 1989.

150. The county's ambulance officers at Courtlands, the Worthing District Heath Authorities Headquarters in Worthing, for Deputy Chief Ambulance Officer David Hook's retirement presentation in 1989.
Back row L/R: Bert Manning, Norman Oakley, Derek Hill, Brian Knight, Brian Attfield, Peter Tidy, David Rice.
Front row L/R: Peter Wells, Pete Williams, Allan Ware, Chief Ambulance Officer Ken Smith, David Hook, Bob Jeffries, John Layhe, Denis Tennent, Jim Boxall.

The National Dispute 1992-1993

151. Chichester Ambulance Station during the dispute over pay and conditions. The dispute began with an overtime ban in September 1989 and went on for months over the winter of 1989/90, during which time the Army were called in to provide emergency cover in some areas.

152. Staff at Bognor Regis Ambulance Station on the picket line during December 1992.

153. Staff at Crawley Ambulance Station on the picket line during the dispute.

154. An army ambulance at Crawley Ambulance Station returning borrowed equipment after the dispute had ended.

155. Staff from Worthing and Shoreham Ambulance Stations held a sponsored ambulance pull along Worthing seafront in October 1990 to raise the money needed to send these two ex service vehicles to Romania.

Yet More For Charity

156. November 1990. Ambulanceman Neil Monery and ambulance woman Helen Davey delivering one of the two ambulances, ex Bognor based Transit, fleet no 229, at Timisoara Hospital, Romania, after driving them across Europe loaded with donated medical supplies.

157. Customline bodied Leyland Daf driver training unit in 1991. It had seating for four in the front cab, driver and instructor and up to two other trainees, while the rear compartment was fitted out as a mobile control unit.

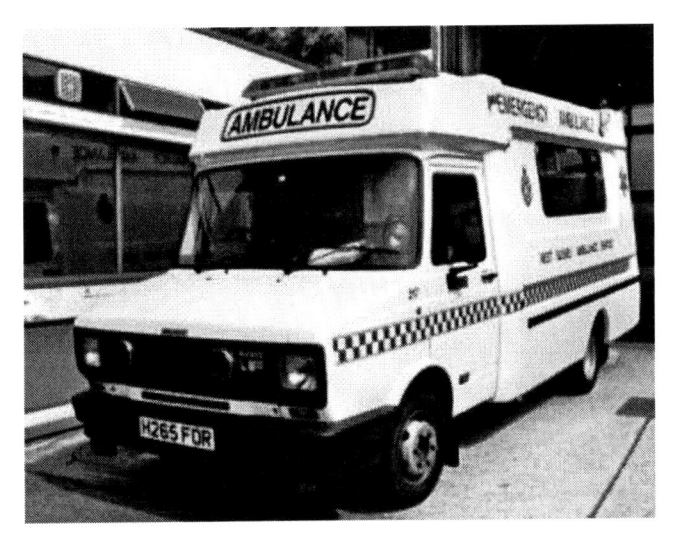

158. Diesel powered Mountain Range bodied Leyland Daf at Bognor Ambulance Station during evaluation trials in 1992.

159. Emergency service crews, including Hotel 900, the Sussex Police Air Support Unit, at the scene of a road traffic accident on the A27 near Patching in 1992. Hotel 900 began operations in 1987, based initially at the Police Headquarters in Lewis, but soon moving to its current base at Shoreham Airport. Paramedics began crewing on a part-time basis from 1988, and as full time crew from January 1991. The aircraft shown, a Bolkow MB109 was able to carry a single stretcher patient alongside the paramedic in the rear cabin. Loading was via the large rear doors at the back of the aircraft.

160. Chief Ambulance Officer Ken Smith handing over the keys to West Sussex Ambulance Services first Paramedic Support Unit, a Ford Mondeo, to Littlehampton based Paramedic Ron Patching at New England College, nr Arundel, in August 1993.
The funds to buy and equip the unit were raised entirely by voluntary donation.

161. The Ambulance Control Room in Summersdale Road, Chichester, after major refurbishment in 1992. This control closed down at 2am on the 2nd February 1997, when the new central control for Sussex Ambulance Service in Lewis took over.

162. Commissioning of the new fleet of Leyland Daf 400 series Customline bodied ambulances at Goodwood House in December 1992. They were fitted with French made Collet easy load trolleys.

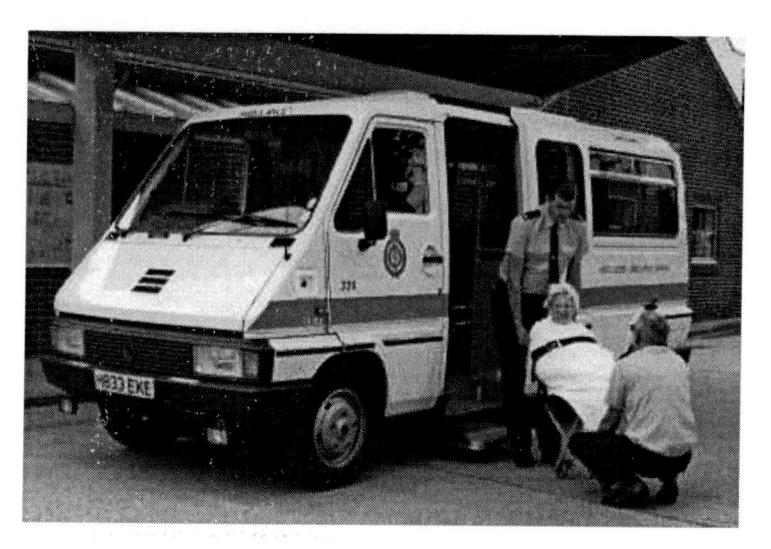

163. Patient Transport Service crew loading a patient into a Renault Master PTS vehicle at Bognor War Memorial Hospital's Day Hospital Unit in 1992.

164. Haywards Heath crews on the forecourt of the town's fire station in February 1993. The ambulances are K895 NRV, Burgess Hill based Leyland Daf 400 and E398 BCD, Haywards Heath based Wadham M.I.A.B. bodied Ford Transit.

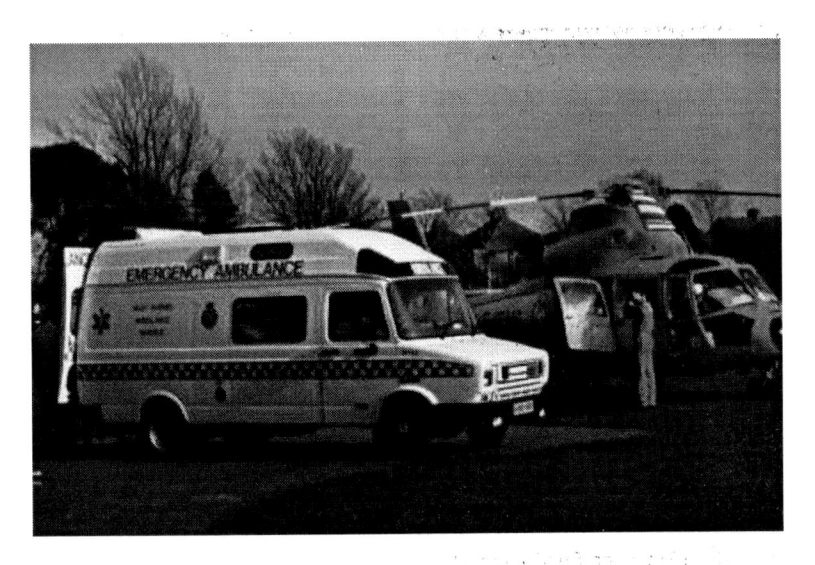

165. Transferring a patient to the Royal London Hospital by air ambulance in March 1993. The London Air Ambulance (HEMS) is at Homefield Park, Worthing, the landing ground for air ambulances immediately adjacent to Worthing Hospital.

Ambulance Trust Meetings

A series of meetings will be held to consult with the public about the proposed West Sussex Ambulance NHS Trust.

It will give the public a chance to find out about the ambulance service and how it will be run in the future.

The Chief Ambulance officer, Ken Smith, will make a presentation and members of his senior management team will be available to answer questions.

They hope to have an ambulance available for public inspection, pressure of work permitting.

Extract from the Observer Newspaper, March 1993.

Operation Angel

166. Ready for the off at Worthing Ambulance Station, December 10th 1993. L/R Organiser Dixie Dean, CAO Ken Smith and team members Bert Greenfield, Gordon Bushell, Jim Vincent, Jo Panchen and Andy Brian.

On the 10th of December 1993, after weeks of frantic preparation six members of the service set out from Brighton as part of Operation Angel, an aid convoy taking aid and medical supplies to the people of the war torn former Republic of Yugoslavia and evacuating civilian casualties from various towns on both sides of the conflict. Led by Sally Becker, the Angel of Mostar, the convoy drove though France and Italy to the port of Ancona and then by ferry across the Adriatic to the Croatian port of Split.

From a base in the coastal village of Donja Brela convoy members distributed aid supplies to hospitals and refugee camps in the area before driving to the border town of Metrkovic to rendezvous with United Nations armoured ambulances that had transported the injured from the devastated and very dangerous town of Mostar some twenty miles away. The casualties were then taken to Split Airport and put on aircraft for flights to various European countries and the USA. The convoy returned to the UK just in time for Christmas.

167. Team members Andy Brian, Jo Panchen and Brian Janman at Donja Brela immediately before setting off to collect the casualties from the UN compound at Metrovic.

1995 - Merger, Trust Status and Amalgamation

WEST SUSSEX AMBULANCE SERVICE
N.H.S.TRUST
4TH WAVE
APPOINTMENT OF NON-EXECUTIVE BOARD MEMBERS

The West Sussex Ambulance Service, which has applied for N.H.S. Trust status from April 1994, is looking for creative, independent minded people with strong commitment to the improvement of patient services in the N.H.S. who can offer enthusiasm and expertise to the Board level. Experience in one or more of the following fields - finance, law, business, community service or senior management, would be particularly welcome.

Non-Executive members of the Trust Board should preferably live or work in West Sussex and would be expected to be available for country wide service for up to three days per month.

The remuneration is £5,000 per annum (subject to deduction of income tax and national insurance).

An information pack and application form are available from:

MR P.J.Wells (Chief Officer)
West Sussex Ambulance Service
Ambulance Headquarters
Southerlands Road,
CHICHESTER West Sussex PO19 8PL
Telephone 0243 552666

Closing date for applications July 5 1993
Interviews will take place in the week commencing July 26 1993

West Sussex Ambulance Service submitted an application for Trust Status to the Secretary of State for Health in 1993. It's stated aims were 'To ensure that the West Sussex Ambulance Service NHS Trust will remain at the forefront of the provision of pre-hospital patient care and health transport services, and to build on the work of recent years to ensure that we continue to provide high quality, accessible services responsive to the particular needs of the population of West Sussex' and 'As an NHS Trust, West Sussex Ambulance Service would remain an integral part of the National Health service, but will benefit from a number of freedoms not available to a Directly Managed Unit'

An extract from the Services Trust application document 'Raising the Standards' goes on to say 'That the Trusts Steering Group believe that an efficient and responsible management structure will lead to a better run Ambulance Service, allowing patients a greater say in the way in which they are treated', and 'Increased operational independence will allow West Sussex Ambulance Service not only to meet the specified requirements of purchasers and staff, but to improve the quality of service to patients, taking account of their individual needs'.

The services application, along with the parallel application made by the East Sussex Ambulance Service, were turned down by the Secretary of State, who considered that a single ambulance trust covering the whole of Sussex would be more appropriate. Consequently a joint application was put forward for consideration and subsequently approved by the Secretary of State, and the new Sussex Ambulance Service NHS Trust, came into being on April 1st 1995.

This service covered the counties of East and West Sussex from its new headquarters in Lewis until, along with both the Surrey and Kent services it too lost its individual county identity and was amalgamated into the newly formed South East Coast Ambulance Service NHS Trust on July 1st 2006.